Beyond The Code

Comprehension and Reasoning Skills

4

Nancy Hall

School Specialty, Inc.

Cambridge and Toronto

Printed in Benton Harbor, MI, in April 2021
ISBN 978-0-8388-2404-7

17 18 19 20 PPG 24 23 22 21

Contents

Review of *Beyond The Code 1, 2,* and *3*

• Draw a line from the word to the picture of the word.

love   school

climb   light

people   head

bedroom   eyes

door   water

Introduction to **Nelson Went Overboard for Dogs**

In many words the **–ed** ending says /ed/ as in *planted*. Sometimes **–ed** says /t/ as in *asked* or /d/ as in *played*.

• Cross out the **–ed** in each word below and write **t** or **d** for the sound the **–ed** makes in that word.

missed __t__   wished _____   stayed _____

loved _____   stopped _____   happened _____

hopped _____   waved _____   slipped _____

More Introduction to **Nelson Went Overboard for Dogs**

- Draw a line to connect the first syllable in the word with the last. Then read these new words from the story. The first one is done for you.

fris   pect
ex   ky
shin   less
steam   ger
ea   ny
rest   ry
wea   ship

- Write the words above next to their meanings.

1. A big boat run by steam = _____

2. To wait for something you know will happen = _____

3. Lively and playful = _____

4. To climb by gripping with legs and hands = _____

5. Tired = _____

6. Wanting very much to do something = _____

7. Never still or quiet = _____

What Does It Mean?

- To go **overboard** means to fall into the _____. It also means to overdo. Which do you think Nelson will do? _____

- You walk down a **gangway** to get off a boat. Read what happens to Nelson on a **gangway**.

- **Glum** means unhappy. Have you ever been **glum**? _____

- A board is a plank of lumber to build with, but to be **bored** means that you _____.

Words for **Nelson Went Overboard for Dogs**

1. **Few** rhymes with *new.*

   There are just a **few** leaves left on the tree.

   Write and spell it: _____

   Crew rhymes with *few* and *new.*

   The **crew** runs the ship.

   Write and spell it: _____

2. **island** = I + lund

   An **island** has water on all sides.

   Write and spell it: _____

3. **most** = mo + st (**Most** rhymes with

   Most of my pals go to my school.

   Write and spell it: _____

   almost = all + **most**

   It is **almost** time for school to begin.

   Write and spell it: _____

4. **Shook** rhymes with *book.*

   Tex **shook** the robot's hand.

   Write and spell it: _____

5. **Their** rhymes with *hair.* (**Their** means belonging to them.)

   Their mittens are too small.

   Write and spell it: _____

Read the word list again.

Words for **Nelson Went Overboard for Dogs**

• Draw a line from each sentence to the picture it goes with.

Our cat is bigger than **their** cat.

Most of the **crew** swam to the **island**.

The dog **shook** itself and got the picnic wet.

We have a **few** computers in our classroom.

Almost everyone likes a sunny day.

Nelson Went Overboard for Dogs!

Nelson's dog Rocko had to stay at home. (By the end of the trip everyone wished Nelson had stayed home, too!) Nelson's mother said that Rocko was too lively and wild to take on a steamship. (But Nelson didn't think so. He loved his dog Rocko.)

As Nelson boarded the steamship for the island of Nantucket with his parents, he was glum. He missed Rocko a lot, and he knew there would be nothing to do on the boat. Besides, he would be bored and lonely without his dog.

Nelson was restless. His dad told him to sit still and look at the seagulls, but Nelson just could not sit still. He needed to be on the go! So when Mom and Dad weren't looking, he slipped away and went down to the lower deck to check things out.

Nelson ran up and down the decks, stepping on feet and tripping over bags. He ran over every inch of that steamship, climbing under seats, swinging on railings, poking under life rafts, and jumping off stairs. One time Nelson even began to shinny up one of the poles that held racks of life vests, until a member of the crew stopped him. Nelson was a very lively fellow!

On this June day there just happened to be lots of dogs on the ship, and Nelson was eager to pat each and every one. He ran all over the ship looking for dogs to meet and greet.

Nelson met all kinds of dogs: tiny dogs, fuzzy dogs, sleepy dogs, frisky dogs, funny-looking dogs . . . and a few flea-bitten dogs! Nelson patted every one. The dogs all liked Nelson. Even the sleepy dogs woke up and wanted to play with him. Some of the dogs wanted to follow Nelson, some began to yelp and whine, and others got all twisted up in leash, feet, and seat! What a tangle! What a racket! For some reason, dogs really seem to like Nelson, and Nelson really likes dogs!

As Nelson was looking for more dogs, he suddenly leaned way out over the side rail to look at a big, shaggy dog on the deck below and almost fell overboard! What a scare! Some people nearby said, "What a close call!" and shook their heads. But Nelson did not care; he just hopped down from the rail and ran on.

By now, Nelson's parents were wondering where he was, and they began to hunt for him. But Nelson was just one step ahead of them. They didn't catch up with him until the boat reached land.

By the time the steamship finally got to Nantucket, everyone on board was very glad that Nelson hadn't fallen overboard. (But they were also glad to see him go!) Most of all, the dog owners were happy to get off the ship for they were weary and needed a rest.

But Nelson was sad to leave the steamship. What a super ride! He had met lots of people and had made lots of new dog pals. He didn't even miss Rocko as much as he expected. As the boat reached the dock, he waved eagerly to everyone, but mostly to the dogs. Then, as Nelson walked down the gangway, he began to itch, and before he knew it, he was itching all over!

Yes **No** **Can't Tell**

• Draw the face to show the answer.

1. Did Nelson leave his dog in the kennel?

2. Can you tell what kind of dog Nelson owns?

3. Did Nelson sit and read a book on the steamship?

4. Did Nelson eat on board the boat?

5. Did Nelson fall overboard into the water?

6. Was the Nantucket steamship bigger than a rowboat?

7. Was Nelson as lively and wild as his dog Rocko?

8. Were the dog owners tired from chasing Nelson?

Why couldn't Nelson sit still? _____

Tell what you think Nelson's parents did on the ship.

_____

How did Nelson feel as he left the steamship? _____

How do you think Nelson behaves in school? _____

_____

Why? _____

Finish the picture of Nelson's dog Rocko.

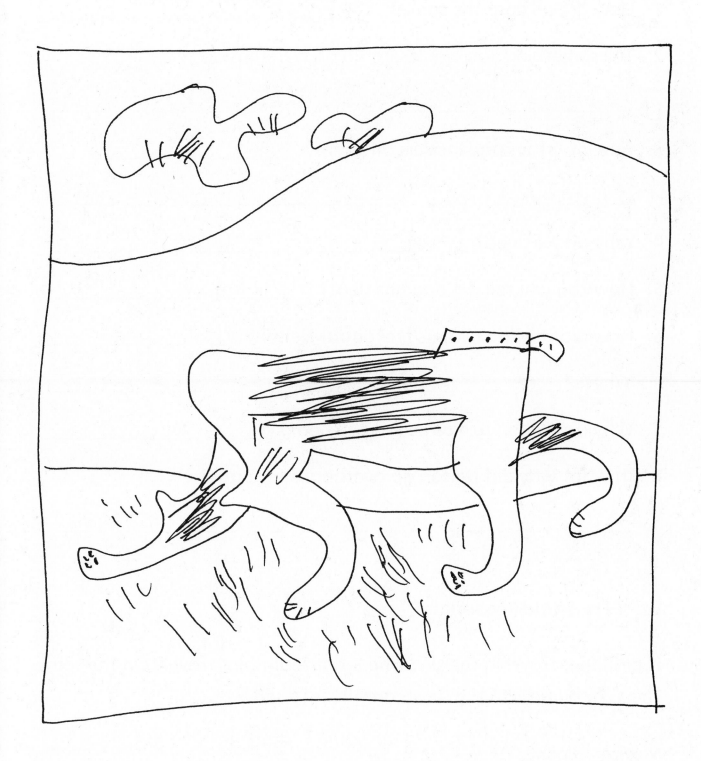

Think About It!

1. How are all dogs the same? _____

2. Tell something you would not do on a steamship.

   _____

3. How are stairs and ladders different? _____

   _____

4. Why do we sleep? _____

5. How can you tell if a dog has fleas? _____

6. How did the dog owners feel about Nelson? _____

   Why? _____

7. Why did Nelson itch as he left the boat? _____

8. In what way did Nelson go overboard for dogs?

   _____

Let's Try Some Reasoning

If airplanes travel in the sky, where do steamships travel? On the sea?
Think: Airplane is to **sky**, as steamship is to **sea**.

Now try this one:
Truck is to **road**, as train is to _____.

Can You Figure This Out?

• Name something that

1. You do not walk on: _____

2. You cannot spill: _____

3. Is not fun to watch: _____

4. You cannot wash: _____

5. Is not a game: _____

6. You cannot cut: _____

7. Is not thrown away: _____

8. Is not yours: _____

Introduction to **What a Scare!**

• Draw a line to connect the first syllable in the word with the last.
  Then read these new words from the story.

shov	nect
con	lop
re	mit
va	el
gal	zing
ad	mind
bla	cant

• Write the words above next to their meanings.

1. On fire; glowing = _____

2. To repeat or tell again = _____

3. To run very fast = _____

4. Something to dig with = _____

5. Empty = _____

6. To attach two things together = _____

7. To say or confess something is true = _____

What Does It Mean?

• To let others **sway** you means to let them tell you what to do.
  Have you ever been **swayed** by anyone? _____

• A **daredevil** is someone who acts in a reckless way.
  Do you know a **daredevil**? _____

• If you do not go any**where**, we say you went <u>no</u>_____.
  Look for the word no**where** at the end of the story and circle it.

14

Words for **What a Scare!**

1. **also** = all + so

   Nina is a good student, and she **also** sings well.

   Write and spell it: _____

   always = all + ways

   No matter when we meet, you are **always** late.

   Write and spell it: _____

2. **behind** = be + hi + nd

   I sit **behind** Rudy in school.

   Write and spell it: _____

3. **burn** = b + er + n

   I got a **burn** on my hand from the hot drink.

   Write and spell it: _____

4. **hold** = h + old

   She **holds** the flag up.

   Write and spell it: _____

5. **who** = Hoo! **Who** rhymes with *two*.

   Who is your pal?

   Write and spell it: _____

6. **How** rhymes with

   How do you play that game?

   Write and spell it: _____

Now read the word list again.

Words for **What a Scare!**

• Draw a line from each sentence to the picture it goes with.

Rex **holds** his cat and puts on its collar.

Who gave you that pen?

I bring the baby inside and **also** my dog.

How can you make a **burn** feel better?

Jenna **always** hides **behind** the apple tree.

What a Scare!

Jake has chores to do inside before he can go out and play baseball. His pal Toby waits on the front steps while Jake sweeps the kitchen and also takes out the trash. When Jake's chores are over at last, he gallops out the front door, tackles Toby, and grabs his baseball cap. The two kids chase each other across the street, while all the time Toby is trying to grab his cap back. These two always have a lot of fun together.

When they get to the vacant lot, Toby stops behind the stone wall and asks, "Want to see what I've got? We can have a blast with these!" He pulls a small box out of his pants pocket and takes out a match. "Let's light the match and play a game. We can see who can hold onto the match the longest." Sometimes Toby is such a daredevil!

"Are you crazy?" Jake yells. "It's stupid to play with fire! Let's go play baseball."

"Come on, Jake! It'll be OK," yells Toby. "We'll be very careful. I know about matches. My dad always lets me light the candles at home."

Jake doesn't agree, but Toby lights the match anyway and lets it burn down low just before blowing it out. Then he lights a second match and hands it quickly to Jake. Jake doesn't know whether to drop it or give it back to his pal. The flame gets lower, and Jake is about to blow it out, but Toby tells him to hold the match for one more second.

"Yikes!" The hot match burns Jake's fingers, and he quickly drops it! But just before the flame goes out, the match lands in some dry grass beside the wall and begins to glow. All of a sudden the dry grass catches fire. They have nothing to put out the flames . . . no water and no shovel to beat out the fire.

In a flash, Toby dashes down the path for home. He yells to Jake to stay there while he runs to get help and a pail of water. It has not rained for weeks so the grass is very dry. In no time the fire is blazing, with more and more grass on fire. The thick smoke makes Jake wheeze and choke.

By now the flames are out of hand! This is a wild blaze! Jake knows he can't do anything by himself. He must get help quickly! So he runs home and yells to Mom.

When Mom sees the smoke across the road, she quickly calls 911. The fire truck is there in no time. The fire crew pulls out the long black hose, connects it, and then begins pumping water. Before long the blaze is out. What a scare!

When they are back home, Mom asks Jake if he knows how the fire began. Jake's teeth and hands are still shaking, and his hair feels like it is standing on end. He cannot speak. He looks away and blinks his eyes. He doesn't really want to admit how it happened. It was stupid of him to play that game with Toby.

At last Jake tells his mom about the match game and how he dropped the match when he felt the hot flame.

"Oh, Jake," she says softly. "Next time you must stop and think before you do something you know is not right." She also reminds him, "You must always remember to use your head and not let others sway you."

Then Mom tells Jake that he must call 911 right away and let them know that he set the fire in the vacant lot by mistake. All of a sudden Jake's eyes begin to water. He sniffs and blows his nose. He can't ever remember feeling this badly. He knows that he is to blame for the fire, and he must admit it.

As he is calling 911, Jake thinks, "I wonder what happened to Toby? Maybe he is bringing a bucket of water right now."

But Toby is nowhere to be seen.

Yes  **No** 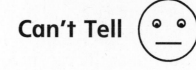 **Can't Tell**

• Draw the face to show the answer.

1. Did Jake want to play with matches?

2. Did Toby also burn his fingers on the lighted match?

3. Did Jake go along with Toby even when he knew not to?

4. Did Toby run away when the grass began to catch on fire?

5. Did Jake have a cold that made him sniff and wheeze?

6. Did the fire crew respond quickly to the 911 call?

7. Was Toby scared and upset about setting the fire?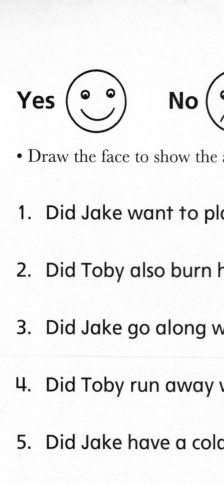

8. Was Mom angry with Jake?

Why did the grass flare up so quickly? _____

What could Jake say to Toby the next time he sees him?

_____

Do you think Jake will ever play with matches again? _____

Has a pal ever asked you to do something you knew wasn't right? _____

Tell what you did and how you felt. _____

_____

24

Finish drawing the picture of Jake as Mom scolds him. Draw his hair and his face. Add a table and a phone to the picture.

Think About It!

1. What can be both stupid and risky? _____

2. How are milk and water different? _____

3. Why did Jake go along with Toby's match game?

   _____

4. What could Jake have done or said to Toby about the game?

   _____

5. Why did Jake sniff and blow his nose as he called 911?

   _____

6. Why didn't Toby come back? _____

7. Did Toby escape blame for helping set the fire? _____

   How would this make you feel if you were Jake? _____

   _____

8. Was Toby a good friend? _____ How do you know?

   _____

   What lesson did Jake learn? _____

Let's Try More Reasoning!

If a ladder is for climbing, what is for sliding? A sled?

Think: Climb is to **ladder**, as slide is to **sled**.

Now try this one:

Ride is to **bike**, as drive is to _____.

Can You Figure This Out?

• How do these things go together?

1. Feet and socks: _____

_____

2. Drum and drumsticks: _____

_____

3. Boat and oars: _____

_____

4. Coat and buttons: _____

_____

5. Pen and paper: _____

_____

6. Bowl and spoon: _____

_____

7. Bike and pedals: _____

_____

Opposites Attract

• Draw a line from the words in the first column to their opposites.

fuzzy	winter
weary	never
risky	many
summer	empty
remember	scream
behind	forget
whisper	ahead
few	sleek
full	safe
always	rested

Review of Plurals

• Plural means more than one. Plurals are made by adding **–s** to a word.

There can be **one insect** or **two insects**. You can read **one book** or **many books**. Make each word below plural by adding **–s**. Then read the words aloud.

cracker	hamster	friend
animal	parakeet	owner
newspaper	lizard	rabbit
roommate	eye	apple
member	suspender	whisker
interest	peanut	parrot

Categories

• Write one word in each box that fits the category at the top and starts
with the letter at the beginning of the line. The first one is done for you.

	Fruit	Clothes	Sports	Colors
R	raspberry			
B				
G				
S				

Review of
3-Syllable Words

• Sometimes 3-syllable words can look hard, but they are not.
Circle the endings **-ed, -ing, -er, -ly,** and **-ful** in the words below.
Then divide the words into syllables, and read the words aloud.

following	skillfully	discovered
chattering	remembered	easily
carefully	dishwasher	beginning
happening	wonderful	reminder

What Am I?

I have a small, thin head and big ears, which help me hear even the faintest creak. My good ears and my keen sense of smell tell me if an enemy is near. My big, soft eyes also help me see very well and give me a sweet look.

• Could I be a rat?

I roam the plains of Africa looking for food, such as grass and leaves. One odd thing about me is my tongue (tung), which is nineteen inches long. I use my tongue to pick the small leaves off tall trees. My thick, gum-like spit protects my lips and tongue from the prickles and spikes of some bushes.

• Could I be a snake?

I have very strong, long, thin legs. When I run, my left front and hind legs move together, then my right front and hind legs. This makes me look as if I am running very, very slowly. But in fact I can outrun a fast pony going more than 30 miles an hour. I can also use my strong legs and feet to beat off an attack.

I am the tallest of all the animals. I am 18 feet tall from head to toe. My neck is also very long, which is why I can reach the topmost leaves of a tall tree.

• Now do you know what I am?

Draw my picture in the box.

Introduction to **A Different Kind of Library**

- Draw a line to connect the first syllable(s) in the word with the last.
  Then read these new words from the story.

care	row
sev • er	taker
li	al
bor	ent
under	bra • ry
dif • fer	lar
pop • u	stand

- Write the words above next to their meanings.

1. A place that loans books to people = _____

2. Well-liked by many people = _____

3. Not alike; not similar = _____

4. A person who takes care of someone or something =
   _____

5. More than two, but not many = _____

6. To take something for a while and then give it back =
   _____

7. To get the meaning of = _____

What Does It Mean?

- To **adopt** means to take into the family and raise as one's _____.

- A **duplex** is a two-family home; it has one family on one side and
  one family on the other _____.

- When you become a member of something, you agree to follow the
  membership rules. Are you a member of anything? _____

Words for **A Different Kind of Library**

1. **work** = wer + k

    We have a lot of **work** to do in school.

    Write and spell it: _____

2. **cage** =

    Bob opens the door of the **cage**.

    Write and spell it: _____

3. **decide** = de + side

    To **decide** means to make up your mind.

    Write and spell it: _____

4. **hurt** = her + t

    If you get **hurt**, you may cry.

    Write and spell it: _____

5. **bright** = **Bright** rhymes with *light*.

    That light is much too **bright**.

    Write and spell it: _____

    tight = **Tight** rhymes with *light*.

    This ring is too **tight** for my finger.

    Write and spell it: _____

    sight = **Sight** rhymes with *light*.

    Sight is one of our five senses.

    Write and spell it: _____

6. **food** = **Food** rhymes with *rude*.

    It is time to give Rover his **food**.

    Write and spell it: _____

Now read the word list again.

Words for **A Different Kind of Library**

• Draw a line from each sentence to the picture it goes with.

Grandma's glasses help her **eyesight**.

I can't **decide** which hat will protect me from the **bright** sun.

Rob **hurt** his leg **working** on the log pile.

This tennis outfit is too **tight**!

The **cage** is locked so I can't give **food** to the pet.

A Different Kind Of Library

    Shandra is a bright nine-year-old who likes to read books, write to pen pals, grow plants, and play soccer. She's also crazy about animals. She loves how soft they feel and how their bright eyes twinkle. Shandra lives in a duplex in Billings, Montana, with her dad and her sixteen-year-old sister Anna. Dad works in the city in a small repair shop fixing cars and trucks, and he doesn't get home until almost seven PM. Shandra and Anna get home from school about the same time, but they don't pal around. Anna spends all her time calling and talking with her friends. Shandra wishes she also had someone to talk to.

In fact, Shandra has lots of things to do after school. To begin with, she fixes herself a big snack. Then she checks the mail and waters her plants, makes her bed, and puts a load in the dishwasher before beginning her homework. At five o'clock she likes to watch "Wild Animal Kingdom." She also sets the table before Dad gets home. Shandra has a lot to do, but, even so, she wishes she had someone to keep her company.

Now Shandra has dreamed about getting a dog or a cat that she could talk to and hold and brush. But cat hair makes her dad sneeze and his eyes get all red and itchy. And Dad says that a dog would be hard to keep in a small duplex. It would also need to go out several times a day. That could be risky in the city!

One day when Shandra is at the library checking out a good animal book to read, she sees a note about another kind of library where you can borrow, not a book, but an animal! It's a pet library run by the local animal shelter.

When Shandra visits the shelter the next day, she discovers that you can get a membership for $5, and then you can borrow a pet for a week. Most of the animals on loan in this library are lost pets or homeless animals that were taken to the shelter after being hurt or lost. Some were given to the shelter by a local pet store when the animals were not sold. The shelter takes in these animals and gives them food, a home, and good care.

Shandra discovers that this is a very different kind of library. For one thing, there is no rule about being silent. (Right now she can hear a parrot chattering "Shelly want a cracker," while a dog in a pen is yapping to get out and run.)

This library also has a rule that a child must be six years or older to borrow a pet, and that a parent must give his or her OK. By the time you are six years old, you can understand that animals need TLC (Tender Loving Care) and may bite if you do not handle them the right way. At this library you can learn to be a good caretaker, and Shandra is eager to learn.

On the other hand, you must pay a $10 fine if you do not take good care of the pet you borrow. But after twenty "good-care" checkouts, you can adopt *any* animal at the library for free! From then on, the animal lives with you and becomes a member of your family. This wonderful library helps people find out what an animal is really like before they decide to keep it for life.

Shandra is thrilled to see all the different animals, and she can't wait to bring Dad here and get his OK to borrow a pet. "It won't hurt to try out a pet for only one week," she tells him at dinner. Anna tells Dad that she will help Shandra take care of it. So after talking it over, Dad agrees.

The following weekend Shandra takes her Dad to the pet library. Together they try to decide on an animal. Would Shandra like to try a lizard or a bunny or a hamster? There is even a little ribbon snake! In fact, there are more than 40 different "critters" to pick from.

"Which one would we like best?" she wonders.

Shandra can't decide which pet to pick. Some of the animals at the library need quite a lot of care, while others are easy to look after and live with. Will she pick Butterscotch, the big, yellow rabbit with long, soft ears that likes to eat clover and spinach? Or Travis, the handsome green lizard? Or Beebe, the shy hamster with the pink nose?

"I'll bet Anna would like to have a tank with a goldfish or a parakeet in a cage," Shandra says to herself.

Shandra learns that rabbits don't like to be picked up, and their legs can scratch. The parakeet sings all the time, which could make it hard to do homework with such a racket. Goldfish and lizards are fun to watch for a little while, but Shandra needs a pet that she can talk to and brush and hold.

Shandra thinks about it for a long time and finally decides to check out Keegan, a sleek, black rat with a long tail who is the most popular animal in the pet library. He is quiet and clean and very interested in people. In fact, he is interested in everything and learns quickly, which makes him fun to watch. Keegan has such a keen sense of smell that his whiskers tremble as he inspects each new thing. He also likes to collect shiny things . . . and then hide them. His eyesight is not the best, but he never misses a trick! And, best of all, he never bites!

But before Shandra can borrow this animal, she must take a test. This is what the test is like. (Can you pass it?)

Check the right one:

When you handle your animal at home, you must:

(a) hold onto it tightly while you run and play.

(b) always sit down while holding it and treat it with care.

(c) put it in your pocket so it can always be near you.

Shandra passes the test easily. She likes animals and she likes reading about their habits. The people at the library tell her she will be a good pet owner someday.

When Shandra checks Keegan out, she is given three things:

1. A basic fact sheet about how rats behave and how to care for them

2. Food for a week

3. A cage with shredded newspaper for the pet to sleep on.

"I can't wait for Keegan to welcome me home from school every day. I know he'll be glad to see me," she whispers to herself. "I'll give him sticks to chew and brush him every day, and Dad will not be bothered by his sleek hair. I think this is the pet for me!"

Shandra carefully picks up Keegan's cage and peeks inside to see if he is cozy. She sees his bright, shiny eyes, and then she begins to giggle. "I think he just winked at me," she says. "What a pet! I know I will want to have Keegan for my roommate for much longer than a week!"

Yes 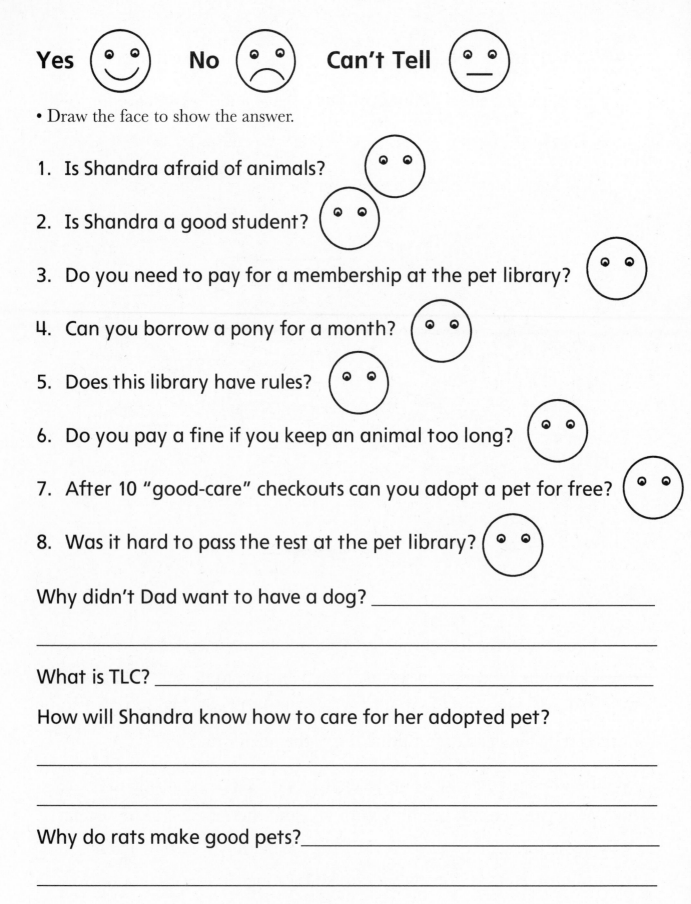 **No** **Can't Tell**

• Draw the face to show the answer.

1. Is Shandra afraid of animals?

2. Is Shandra a good student?

3. Do you need to pay for a membership at the pet library?

4. Can you borrow a pony for a month?

5. Does this library have rules?

6. Do you pay a fine if you keep an animal too long?

7. After 10 "good-care" checkouts can you adopt a pet for free?

8. Was it hard to pass the test at the pet library?

Why didn't Dad want to have a dog? _____

_____

What is TLC? _____

How will Shandra know how to care for her adopted pet?

_____

_____

Why do rats make good pets?_____

_____

Finish the picture of the pet library by drawing cages for the animals and adding eyes where they are missing.

Think About It!

1. How are a washer and a dishwasher different? _____

   _____

2. Why don't animals wear clothes? _____

3. Name an animal that looks like a lizard, but is much bigger.

   _____

4. Why is it risky to have a dog or cat in the city? _____

   _____

5. Why was Keegan the rat so popular? _____

   _____

6. How did Shandra feel as she was deciding which pet to borrow?

   _____

7. How can you tell which animal is right for your family?

   _____

8. Which animal would you borrow if you could? _____

   Why? _____

Let's Try More Reasoning!

Peanuts are to **crunchy**, as gum is to _____.

Think: Peanuts are **crunchy**, and gum is _____.

Now try these:

Grass is to **green**, as sky is to _____.

Kitten is to **soft**, as stone is to _____.

Can You Figure This Out?

• Name 3 things you know that are

1. Soft: _____

2. Slow: _____

3. Bright: _____

4. Sticky: _____

5. Striped: _____

6. Metal: _____

7. Locked: _____

Introduction to **A Birthday to Remember**

- Draw a line to connect the first syllable in the word with the last. Then read these new words from the story.

whis	vet
mi • cro	ent
ped	ber
re • mem	per
won • der	al
pres	wave
vel	ful

- Write the words above next to their meanings.

1. Very fine and grand = _____

2. To move your feet on a bike = _____

3. A gift = _____

4. A soft, thick fabric = _____

5. An oven that cooks quickly = _____

6. To bring back to mind; not forget = _____

7. To speak very softly = _____

What Does It Mean?

- "It didn't **bother** him" means it did not _____.

- If I give you three bucks, I give you $_____.

- To **plead** means to beg someone. Find out who **pleaded** in this story.

- If I **agreed** with you, I would say _____.

48

Words for **A Birthday to Remember**

1. **girl** = g + er + l.

The new **girl** is tall and thin.

Write and spell it: _____

2. **first** = f + er + st

First prize is a blue ribbon.

Write and spell it: _____

3. **birthday** = b + er + th + day
My **birthday** cake has ten candles.

Write and spell it: _____

4. **dollar** = doll + er
I have five **dollars** in my piggy bank.

Write and spell it: _____

5. **again** = u + g + en

Can you write your name **again**?

Write and spell it: _____

6. **noon** rhymes with *moon*.
The sun can be very bright at **noon**.

Write and spell it: _____

afternoon = after + noon
The game will be played this **afternoon**.

Write and spell it: _____

Now read the word list again.

Words for **A Birthday to Remember**

• Draw a line from each sentence to the picture it goes with.

Rachel got ten **dollars** on her **first birthday**.

At the **noon** picnic the tiger ate too much.

He must take the driving test **again**.

It was a super **afternoon** for a sail.

The tiny **girl** cannot reach the bike pedals.

A Birthday to Remember

Alvin didn't know what to get his mom for her birthday. She could use so many things, like a new dress, a color TV, and a microwave oven. But what could he get with the money he had in his piggy bank? At first he wanted to get her some silver earrings . . . or maybe a pink hairbrush? Or a pair of red velvet slippers? She would also like a shiny new cake pan. Alvin had saved three dollars of his own money to spend for Mom's birthday present. He wanted her birthday to be really super this year. A birthday she would always remember!

It was a very hot afternoon as Alvin rode his bike to go shopping at the stores on Main Street. It was really too hot to ride a bike in that West Texas sun, but it did not bother Alvin. He looked in all the windows and went into several stores. Everything seemed to cost a lot! But Alvin knew that sometimes there are sales so he kept looking. He spent all afternoon hunting for something that Mom would like, but he didn't see anything. Everything cost too much!

"Why can't I find something I like for three bucks?" Alvin wondered, as he left the shopping streets and began to bike slowly back home again. He needed a cool present for his mom but one that did not cost more than three dollars!

Still thinking about what to do, he began to pedal more slowly. He had wanted this to be such a wonderful birthday for Mom. What could he do? Where could he look?

Then, Alvin saw a tall, thin girl coming down the street holding a big basket. "Do you want a free kitten?" she asked him when he got nearer. "We need to find good homes for them. We have too many kittens, you see, and we can't feed them all. They are very sweet. Please," the girl pleaded. "I must find good homes for all of them. How about taking two?"

The kittens were so cute and playful that Alvin just had to put down his bike and look at them. He liked the black one with a white patch on its nose. This kitten seemed to know it, too, for it jumped up on the side of the basket and flipped over, landing smack in Alvin's hands. It seemed like this kitten had chosen Alvin!

Alvin patted the tiny kitten and held it close for a second. Then he remembered that last month his mom had said that she had always wanted a cat. The next thing he knew he had agreed to take the black kitten home with him. It was so funny and soft and cuddly, and besides, it needed a good home!

"My mom will like this present best of all," Alvin whispered to himself as he rode home with the black kitten carefully tucked on top of his jacket in the bike basket. "Mom has always wanted a cat, and we will be helping other people by taking it. Now I can use my three bucks to get some cat food." He smiled as he patted the soft bundle again. "I wonder what Mom will name it?" he said to himself.

This *would* be a birthday to remember, after all!

Yes 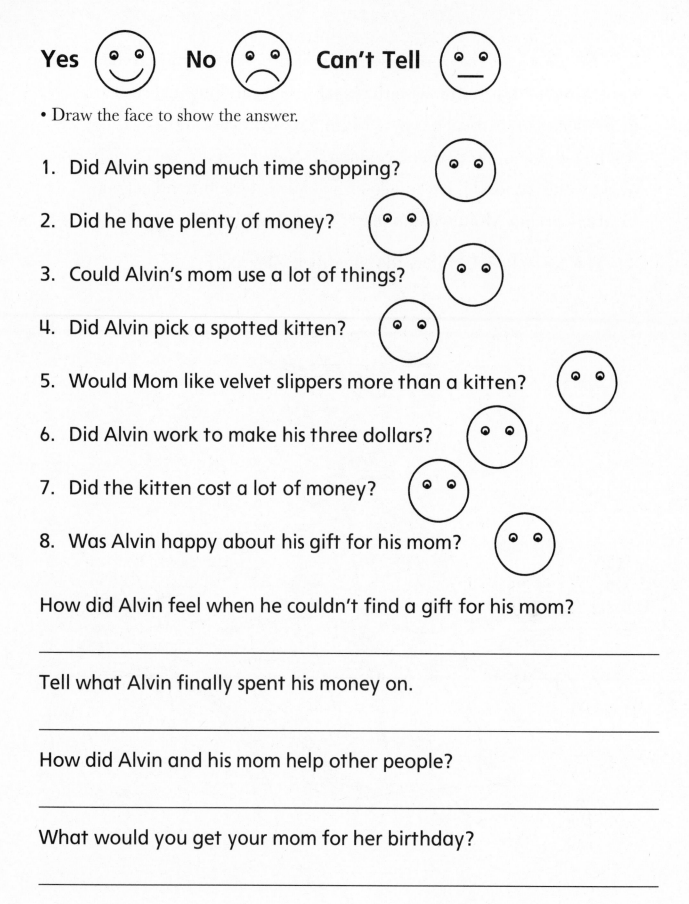 **No** **Can't Tell**

• Draw the face to show the answer.

1. Did Alvin spend much time shopping?

2. Did he have plenty of money?

3. Could Alvin's mom use a lot of things?

4. Did Alvin pick a spotted kitten?

5. Would Mom like velvet slippers more than a kitten?

6. Did Alvin work to make his three dollars?

7. Did the kitten cost a lot of money?

8. Was Alvin happy about his gift for his mom?

How did Alvin feel when he couldn't find a gift for his mom?

_____

Tell what Alvin finally spent his money on.

_____

How did Alvin and his mom help other people?

_____

What would you get your mom for her birthday?

_____

Finish the picture showing what Alvin saw in the basket.

Think About It!

1. How are all ovens the same? _____

2. How are a bike and a truck different? _____

_____

3. Why do we have sidewalks? _____

_____

4. Name one thing Alvin could buy with three dollars. _____

_____

5. Why didn't Alvin walk to the stores? _____

_____

6. If you don't have money to buy a present, what can you do?

_____

7. Why was Alvin so happy about the present he got his mom?

_____

8. How else could the girl find good homes for the kittens?

_____

Let's Try More Reasoning

Saw is to **cut**, as hammer is to _____.

Think: A saw is something that **cuts**;

a hammer is something that _____.

Now try these:

Pen is to **write**, as crayon is to _____.

Oven is to **bake**, as freezer is to _____.

Can You Figure This Out?

• How are these the same?

1. Sidewalk and street: _____

_____

2. Belt and suspenders: _____

_____

3. Toaster and oven: _____

_____

4. Button and zipper: _____

_____

5. Peas and beans: _____

_____

6. Bell and siren: _____

_____

7. Brother and sister: _____

_____

8. School and library: _____

_____

Who Am I?

• Read the clues. Then write the name of the person or animal you met in this book. The names are listed below.

1. I like to ride my bike, but shopping is hard.

   Who am I? _____

2. I like dogs, but I don't like fleas.

   Who am I? _____

3. I like animals that I can talk to and brush and hold.

   Who am I? _____

4. I am yellow and have soft ears. Who am I? _____

5. I let my pal talk me into something I shouldn't have done.

   Who am I? _____

6. I am having a birthday. Who am I? _____

7. I have bright eyes, but my eyesight is weak.

   Who am I? _____

8. I ran when the fire began and I didn't come back.

   Who am I? _____

Keegan   **Nelson**   **Shandra**   **Mom**

Alvin   **Jake**   **Butterscotch**   **Toby**

Opposites Attract

• Draw a line from the words
  in the first column to their opposites.

first	solid
different	lend
work	tiny
hungry	full
hollow	last
immense	play
risky	dull
bright	midnight
borrow	same
noon	safe

Categories

• Write one word in each box that fits the category at the top and starts
  with the letter at the beginning of the line.

	Wild Animals	Vegetables	States	Desserts
P				
A				
C				
T				

Review of 3-Syllable Words

• Circle the endings: **-en, -ed, -ing, -er** in the words below.
  Then divide each word into syllables, and read the words aloud.

forbidden	collecting	pretending
insisted	endangered	storyteller
easier	reflected	explaining

Review of Plurals

• Make each word plural by adding **-s.** Then read the words.

lifejacket	prayer	whitecap
peanut	bottle	bumblebee
ripple	sneaker	pancake

What Am I?

I spend much of my life in or near swamps and rivers. Most of the time I like to lie still and doze in the sun or hide in the mud of the riverbed.

• Am I a salamander?

My big, bulky, bumpy body is 18 feet long! With my wide head and thick, stubby legs I can top 500 lbs. on the scale. My tail is very long and strong, which makes me glide fast in water, but I am slow and clumsy on land.

• Am I a water buffalo?

My jaw is long and wide and my teeth are strong. I have a mean grin, which makes people fear me, but I just eat frogs and fish. At times I catch and eat a snake or a salamander. I lay my eggs in a nest of damp grass and mud; then I leave. As the nest rots, the wet grass gives off heat, which helps hatch my eggs within three months. Then each 8-inch baby is on its own and must make its way into the water to take care of itself. Each baby will grow one foot a year for six years until it is a full-grown adult.

• How many feet am I when I am full grown?

For many years my skin was used to make belts, shoes, and handbags. I was hunted until I nearly became extinct. In the 1950s, people could not hunt or kill me, and those who did were put in jail. Now I am no longer endangered.

• Now do you know what I am?

Draw my picture in the box.

Introduction to **The Treasure Hunt**

• Draw a line to connect the first syllable in the word with the last.
  Then read the new words from this story.

ap	cate
pre	sins
hol	pear
hun	lot
lo	tend
rai	low
pi	gry

• Write the words above next to their meanings.

1. Wanting or needing food = _____

2. To come into sight = _____

3. Having nothing inside = _____

4. One who takes an airplane up in the air. _____

5. Small, sweet, dried grapes = _____

6. To find the place or track it down = _____

7. To act as if something is real when it is not = _____

What Does It Mean?

• A **bandana** is something you put over your _____.

• When you send a letter, you put it in an **envelope**, address it, and
  then put on a _____.

• A **clearing** in the woods is a place that has no _____.

• To **insist** means to demand. If you insist on doing something again,
  you would say, _____.

64

Words for The Treasure Hunt

1. **round** = r + out + nd

   This O is **round**.

   Write and spell it: _____

   around = u + round

   Luke walked **around** the sleeping tiger.

   Write and spell it: _____

2. **friend** = fr + end

   A **friend** is a pal that you trust.

   Write and spell it: _____

3. **clue** = **Clue** rhymes with *blue*.

   The spy finds a **clue** to the puzzle.

   Write and spell it: _____

4. **place** = **Place** rhymes with *chase*.

   We have rented a **place** by the lake.

   Write and spell it: _____

5. **treasure** = trez + ure

   Rosa finds the **treasure** chest.

   Write and spell it: _____

6. **woods** = would + s (**Wood** rhymes with *good*.)

   There are a lot of pine trees in the **woods**.

   Write and spell it: _____

Now read the word list again.

Words for **The Treasure Hunt**

• Draw a line from each sentence to the picture it goes with.

Let's build a **place** in the **woods** for our club to meet.

The **treasure** chest is full of money.

The fingerprint was the first **clue** to the robbery.

My **friend** will go to the library.

This belt can go **around** my waist.

The Treasure Hunt

It was a hot Sunday afternoon in July. My family was spending the week with our friends, the Rizzos, at their cabin in the woods in Wisconsin. For several days we had lots of fun playing games, jumping over logs, climbing trees, swinging from branches, pretending to be pilots, collecting stones, and even picking milkweed pods.

But then Tony and I were bored. We wanted to do something new and different. But what could it be? Our fifteen-year-old sisters, Judy and Eva, said they could help. They would send us on a treasure hunt to find a hidden prize. What fun! Sometimes our sisters were the best!

We were eager to begin the hunt right away. But first Judy and
Eva had to write clues and then hide them along with the treasure.
While we waited for the hunt to begin, we stuffed our pockets with
peanut butter crackers in case we got hungry later. But still our sisters
did not come back. Now we began to think the treasure hunt would
never happen! Where were those girls?

At noon Tony's sister Eva appeared with an envelope and handed it to me. It was our job to follow the clues and locate the spot where the treasure was hidden. We knew this would be easy and lots of fun.

Here is the first clue:

In the woods there is a hollow place in a tree that holds a small box. This place is damp and low. Here you will find the second clue. Good luck hunting!

"That must be the hollow tree that we call the 'unk-water' tree," yelled Tony. "Follow me; I know the way there!" (We ran into the woods yelling, "Let's go! Let's go! But don't go slow! No, no, no!")

Tony was right. In a hole near the bottom of an old oak tree was a tiny box. He handed it to me, and I opened it quickly. Inside was Clue 2:

Do you hear water rushing? Now look for the biggest rock, and the next clue will be hidden there. Good luck hunting!

"Is there a stream in these woods?" I asked.

Tony nodded his head. "It's a long hike to the other side of the woods beyond the clearing. I think that must be the place. There is no rushing water any other place," he insisted.

"Let's go there then!" I yelled. I knew Tony must be right for he had spent many summers here.

It was cool and shady hiking in the woods until we got to the clearing where the hot sun was beating down on us. We were very hungry so it was a good thing we had plenty of crackers with us. (But why didn't we bring a water bottle?) Tony kept wiping his head with a bandana, and I panted like a big shaggy dog. Only the bumblebees buzzing in and out of the milkweed plants did not seem to be bothered by the heat!

On the other side of the clearing Tony yelled to me, "Do you hear it? It's rushing water! We must be close!"

The stream was rushing swiftly over the stones, and in the middle was the biggest rock I had ever seen. We climbed up on top of the big rock and looked all around. No clue! This hunt was not so easy after all!

"Let's wade in the stream to cool off," I said. As we were splashing beneath the big rock, I looked up and saw paper sticking out of a crack in the rock. It was clue 3:

Walk past the weeping willow tree and down the path. Take a right at the bottom of the hill. When you reach something old and broken-down, open it, and look inside.

As always, Tony said that he knew where to go to find something old and broken-down: Nory's old hunting shack, but it was a long hike to get there. This time I did *not* agree with my friend Tony. This could be *any* old thing . . . an old cave, an old lean-to, an old stump, or an old shed. (Most of all, I didn't want to go on another long hike.)

"What if we go all that way and then discover there is no clue. Besides, it's *so* hot!" I groaned. At last I agreed that the shack *could* be the place. So off we went, a bit more slowly this time.

When we got to the old shack we were very tired. "Let's have a rest after we take a look inside," I hinted.

"Why did our sisters make this treasure hunt so long?" Tony asked as he slowly opened the broken door. We looked down at the sagging boards under our feet, and there was another envelope with our names on it. This time Tony tore it open and it said:

This is the last clue! There is a stone wall behind our cabin. Follow it into the woods until you see something red. There you will find what you are looking for! You are very good treasure hunters!

In a flash we forgot we were tired. We ran back to the cabin and went behind it to the stone wall. Walking slowly, we looked up and down, in and out, and all around. Something red? What could that be? A flag? A kite? A beach ball? A book? A bag of candy?

"Look!" I yelled. "Over there by those bushes . . . under those newspapers!" Tony gave a poke with a stick and out fell a big, red treasure chest. Inside were two packs of gum, a bottle of soap bubbles, a jump rope, two shiny red apples, two boxes of raisins, and a big bag of peanuts in the shell. What a super treasure! Our sisters knew what we liked best. We were so hungry that we ate the treats up in no time. Yum! Yum!

Sometimes our sisters were so cool!

Yes  **No** **Can't Tell**

• Draw the face to show the answer.

1. Did the kids have fun swinging from the branches?

2. Did Tony and his pal forget to pack snacks?

3. Do you find "unk-water" in a hollow tree?

4. Did Tony always know where to go?

5. Was Tony's friend in this story a girl?

6. Did the bumblebees get angry from the heat and sting?

7. Was the treasure hunt a long one?

8. Did the two sisters get hot and tired hiding the clues?

How many clues did the kids find in all? _____

What was the best thing in the treasure chest? _____

What would you like to find in a treasure chest? _____

Think of one word that describes the sisters. _____

Draw what the kids found in the treasure chest.

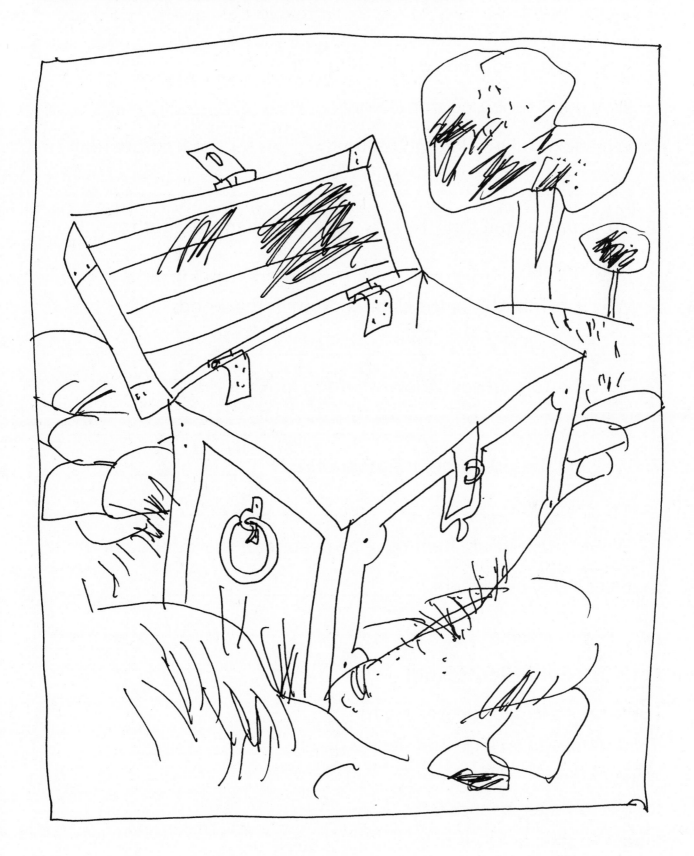

Think About It!

1. How are a stream and a lake different? _____

2. Why don't rocks and stones float? _____

3. Why did it take so long to set up the clues for the treasure hunt?

    _____

4. How can you tell that the kids were hot when they got to

    the clearing? _____

5. Why was it hotter in the clearing than in the woods?

    _____

6. How did Tony always know where to look for clues?

    _____

7. Why did the kids forget they were tired? _____

    _____

8. Would the treasure hunt have been easier if the kids had had

    bikes? Why or why not? _____

    _____

Let's Try Some Reasoning!

Pants are to **legs,** as sleeves are to _____.

Think: Pants go on **legs,** and sleeves go on _____.

Now try these:

Ring is to **finger,** as sock is to _____.

Plug is to **sink,** as key is to _____.

Can You Figure This Out?

1. Name an animal that

   lives in the woods: _____

   lives underground: _____

   is extinct: _____

   is a pet: _____

2. Name a bird that

   is blue: _____

   clucks: _____

   is tiny: _____

   is very big: _____

3. Name something you would eat

   for lunch: _____

   as a snack: _____

   on your birthday: _____

   at a ball game: _____

4. Name something you would put on

   to go to school: _____

   to go jogging: _____

   to go sledding: _____

   to go to bed: _____

5. Name a way you could travel

   to school: _____

   to visit a nearby pal: _____

   across the sea: _____

   to work: _____

Introduction to **A Wild Ride**

• Draw a line to connect the first syllable in the word with the last.
  Then read these new words from the story.

ex	cure
sail	ty
out	mense
se	ral
plen	plain
im	or
spi	line

• Write the words above next to their meanings.

1. Tell the meaning of = _____

2. Very, very big = _____

3. More than one needs = _____

4. To make safe by tying up well = _____

5. The outer shape or profile = _____

6. Twisting = _____

7. A person who works on a boat = _____

What Does It Mean?

• A **prism** is a glass object that reflects light.

  Have you seen a **prism**? _____

• A **roller-coaster** ride is one that goes up and _____.

• If you **bail** a boat, you take water out of it with a pail or a

  _____.

• To be **tense** means to feel uptight and _____.

Words for **A Wild Ride**

1. **far** = **Far** rhymes with
   We must travel **far** from home.

   Write and spell it: _____

2. **excited** = ex + si + ted
   The fans were **excited** at the soccer game.

   Write and spell it: _____

3. **story** = st + or + E
   The **story** is fun to read.

   Write and spell it: _____

4. **high** = hi (**High** rhymes with *sky*.)
   The flagpole is very **high**.

   Write and spell it: _____

5. **house** = how + s
   Our **house** is white with a black door.

   lighthouse = light + **house**
   A **lighthouse** helps ships see in the rain and fog.

   Write and spell it: _____

6. **Michigan** = Mish + e + gan
   Michigan is a state in the U.S.

   Write and spell it: _____

Now read the word list again.

Words for **A Wild Ride**

• Draw a line from each sentence to the picture it goes with.

The **lighthouse** sends a beam of light as a signal.

The class is **excited** to read the **story** about the monster.

My **house** is located in the middle of the city.

It is not too **far** to drive from Boston to **Michigan**.

Max thinks the tree is too **high** to climb.

A Wild Ride

My granddad lives with us and he is such a good storyteller. He tells many good tales. The ones I like best are about our Mom when she was a kid.

"Please, Gramp, tell us a story!" my brother Lee and I beg him at bedtime. "Tell us about when Mom was a little girl."

"Well, let's see, did I ever tell you about the time that we were nearly lost at sea? Your mom was just about twelve years old," said Gramp.

"Tell us, tell us!" we yell.

This is granddad's story.

One summer, many years ago in Michigan, your mom and her pal Isabel were playing on the beach. As they looked out across the big lake, they could see Beaver Island and they wondered what it was like out there. How they wished they could find out! That night your mom asked me if I would take them there in my boat.

"No, dear Rachel, that's much too far away for a small boat like mine," I said, "but maybe we can go to the lighthouse at Skillagalee some time. It's much closer. Perhaps Isabel's dad would like to come along, too.

Your mom was very excited just thinking about that trip. She never stopped talking about it. I told her that before setting out we needed a fair sky and no wind. She knew the old saying "Red sky at night, sailor's delight."

"The sky must really be **red** at dusk for the next day to be good for boating," I told her. So every night she watched for a red sky.

A few days later, as we sat eating our pancakes, your mom said, "There was a red sky last night, right? So how about that boat trip today, Dad?

"You're right, Rachel. This would be a fine day. Let's go," I said. "Will you call Isabel and her dad?"

Isabel and Rachel could hardly wait to see a real lighthouse and meet the lighthouse keeper. (In those days, every lighthouse had a keeper who lived on the island to take care of the light and see that it was always clean and shining brightly at night so that ships wouldn't hit the rocks.)

We quickly packed two water bottles, a box of crackers, some trail mix, and a peach for each of us so we would have plenty to eat on the trip. Rachel was in such a rush to get going that she left her sneakers and baseball cap and had to run back to get them. (Bare feet are forbidden on a boat trip.) Telling Mom that we'd be back for lunch, she ran down to the beach where Mr. Linden, Isabel, and I were waiting with the boat.

My old skiff was just 14 feet long and well built with a brand new motor, but I told Rachel and Isabel to bring the oars, just in case. I also insisted that they both put on lifejackets before getting into the boat.

Skillagalee Island is about five miles offshore in Lake Michigan, but I knew it would take some time to get there in my boat. So we all sang songs and told jokes, and the girls played "Who Am I?" (Your mom was such a good player. She could always think of the right name by the second clue.)

When Isabel and Rachel got a bit restless, we ate the crackers and trail mix. That hit the spot, but then our throats were so dry that we drank all the water and ate the peaches as well. Then the two girls began dragging their sticky fingers in the water to make ripples. "Don't lean over so far! You could fall in," Mr. Linden told them.

I think Isabel was the first to spot the island. "There's the outline of a lighthouse over there," she called. "It must be Skillagalee." What a welcome sight it was! Our legs were stiff, and the girls were eager to get off and run.

As we landed I saw that the sky was getting a bit gray. The old lighthouse keeper came down to the shore to greet us and help us secure our lines tightly. His eyes were twinkling as he shook hands and told us his name was Skipper Swain. He was always glad to see people, for he lived alone on this island with his cat Drummer.

Skipper Swain wanted to show us the place. "How about a quick trip around the lighthouse?" he asked with a grin. "I'll show you how the big light works!"

We agreed that it would be fun, but it had to be a *quick* trip. Mr. Linden and I had decided to head back home before too long as the sky was getting grayer and grayer.

Your mom and Isabel ran ahead up the steep, iron steps of the lighthouse. Like all spiral stairs, there were many tiny steps twisting round and round to the top. It made you feel dizzy to climb them so fast. We decided that a lighthouse keeper must be in very good shape to handle stairs like these every day. The skipper grinned at this.

On the top at last, we saw the big lens. It was immense and very shiny and bright with many small glass prisms all around it. The prisms reflected the light and made it even brighter. It was fun to hear the skipper explain how he had to wipe all the little prisms to keep the light clear and bright.

We thanked Skipper Swain for our visit and quickly set off for home in our small boat. The wind was stronger now, and we could see a few whitecaps offshore.

I'll never forget that trip home. It was like a roller-coaster ride, with the boat rocking up and down in the biggest waves I had ever seen. At times I had to stand up to steer the boat. Each wave that came at us was so high that I couldn't see past it. On each dip the wind also drove some water over the sides of the boat. Mr. Linden yelled to the girls to help him bail. Using their baseball caps, they dipped water out of the boat as fast as they could. We all got very wet and cold.

Your mom asked grimly, "How deep is Lake Michigan?" as she looked down into the water. I knew she was beginning to feel scared! Mr. Linden told her the lake was about 300 feet deep. That *was* a long way down! She looked very green and seasick. I felt badly for her.

Now it was getting foggy, and we could just see the shore. The two girls were scared, and I felt a bit tense myself. My hands began to shake. We were still a long way from land. I think just about then we all said a few silent prayers.

Well, you know the ending! We made it back home safely. It was so good to feel land under our feet as we climbed off the boat! Your grandma was down on the beach looking for us. She gave us all big hugs. We knew we were lucky to be back home!

Granddad's eyes were misty as he came to the end of the story. "I will never forget that trip to Skillagalee so many years ago and the lesson we *all* learned that wild day: small boats are for small trips, and not for high seas.

Yes  **No**  **Can't Tell**

• Draw the face to show the answer.

1. Did the kids want to take a sailboat to the lighthouse?

2. Was Skillagalee closer to shore than Beaver Island?

3. Did Mom tell Rachel to put on her sandals?

4. Was the lighthouse easy to get to?

5. Did Skipper Swain want them to stay for supper?

6. Did Isabel and Rachel help bail out the boat?

7. Was Dad scared that the boat would tip over?

8. Was everyone glad to get back home safely?

What game was Rachel so good at playing? _____

What did the lighthouse look like? _____

_____

What was the name of Skipper Swain's cat? _____

What did the girls use to bail out the boat? _____

What else can you use to bail out a boat? _____

Finish drawing the picture of Skipper Swain and his cat.

Think About It!

1. How are an apple and a peach different? _____

_____

2. What can be both cold and wet? _____

3. Why is it hard to be in a boat in the fog? _____

_____

4. Why did Rachel forget her sneakers? _____

_____

5. How do we know that Skipper Swain was fit and well? _____

_____

6. How do we know Rachel was scared of the big waves? _____

_____

7. How did the prisms make the light brighter? _____

_____

8. What would have made the trip to Skillagalee safer or less scary?

_____

Let's Try Some Reasoning!

Sing is to **song**, as read is to _____.

Campfire is to **hot**, as snowball is to _____.

Eat is to **cake**, as drink is to _____.

Hat is to **head**, as shoe is to _____.

Can You Figure This Out?

1. Dad went to the store. When he came out, the door of his car was dented. What could have happened? _____

_____

2. When we went outside to play, we discovered that our rope swing was broken. What could have happened? _____

_____

3. Mom was in the kitchen fixing toast and oatmeal for us to eat. As we came down the stairs we smelled smoke. What could have happened? _____

_____

4. I opened my wallet to pay for the donut, and there was no money. What could have happened? _____

_____

5. My sister said she would make a surprise for us after school, but when we got home she wasn't there. What could have happened?

_____

_____

6. As I was walking home from the school bus stop, I discovered I had no notebook. What could have happened? _____

_____

7. When we got home Dad was closing all the doors and windows. What could have happened? _____

_____

Who Is It?

• Draw a line from the person or animal in the stories to the word
  or words that describe him or her.

Gramp	hot and weary
Mom who called 911	itchy
Nelson	saw the island first
Rachel	a good storyteller
Toby with the matches	too lively and wild
Shandra	reckless
Rocko the dog	an animal lover
Skipper Swain	fit from climbing stairs
Isabel	quietly upset
Tony and his pal	"cool" and "the best"
Judy and Eva, the sisters	seasick and scared

Words Introduced in **Beyond The Code 4**

afternoon	dollar	lighthouse
again	excited	Michigan
almost	far	most
also	few	noon
always	first	place
around	food	round
behind	friend	shook
birthday	girl	sight
bright	high	story
burn	hold	their
cage	house	tight
clue	how	treasure
crew	hurt	who
decide	island	woods